FINISHING LINE PRESS

www.finishinglinepress.com

Stitches

poems by

Sarah Cummins Small

Finishing Line Press
Georgetown, Kentucky

Stitches

ACKNOWLEDGMENTS

Gratitude to the editors of the following publications, where some of the poems
in this collection first appeared:

Acorn Whistle, "Boneless Skinless"
Appalachia Bare, "Spring on Chestnut Top"
Breathing the Same Air: An East Tennessee Anthology, "Seventeen Hours, Give or
Take" and "Driving Up Unaka Mountain"
Cider Press Review, "Where Emily Leapt"
Free the Verse, "Ironing Lessons"
Knoxville Writers Guild, "Inheritance" and "Strawberry Moon in June"
Migrants & Stowaways: An Anthology of Journeys, "The Botanist and His Wife"
Pure Slush, "Rock of Ages"
Re/View, "Coming Out of the Den"
Willawaw Journal, "Life Cycle" and "Unstitched"
Willow Review, "War"
Yalobusha Review, "Dad, Peeling Apples"

Publisher: Leah Huete de Maines
Editor: Christen Kincaid
Cover Art and Design: Summer Small
Author Photo: Donna Williams
Cover Design: Elizabeth Maines McCleavy

Order online: www.finishinglinepress.com
also available on amazon.com

Author inquiries and mail orders:
Finishing Line Press
PO Box 1626
Georgetown, Kentucky 40324
USA

Contents

To my father and mother,
whose stories are forever stitched upon my heart

To my botanist and our three, with love and squalor always

"*O what we gather and O Lord
bless what we pass on.*"
—*Tyree Daye, "Inheritance"*

"*Esperanza smiled and reached over and gently pulled the yarn,
unraveling the uneven stitches. Then she looked into Isabel's trusting
eyes and said, 'Do not ever be afraid to start over.'*"
—*Pam Muñoz Ryan, Esperanza Rising*

War

Our mother is beautiful
without makeup, with the round balls
of her cheekbones like crabapples
or plums, and her crooked front
tooth. But with a little
pencil to shade in the sharp arch
of eyebrows and bright red lipstick, she becomes
a black-and-white
photograph hung in a young man's barracks
where in the early evening before dark
and after a green supper, one soldier lies
sideways on his cot facing her,
tracing the soft outline of her cheek
with one knuckle, three fingers from his lips
to hers and back. We will never be
so carefully memorized.

Inheritance

We came into it all
without breaking of glass, or lifting
of veil, or a grandmother's cameo
ring. No family heirlooms
in our first rented house; instead
we depended on thrift store end tables,
a lamp, a couch. We wished

for chipped dishes that told
a great-aunt's rich history
of struggle and survival. We were lonely
without a background, without cabbage
or latkes or black-eyed peas.
We ease into it

year by year. I learn to quilt,
meticulously stitching
my initials in a corner; he builds a cradle,
a stool, a wooden horse. We resurrect
dead relatives through our children
naming them John and Alice and Henry.
and record each birth in a fat
white Bible. They are the first

to grace its tissue-thin pages,
though my handwriting lacks
the necessary elegance, the gentle curves
of a practiced pen. The house we choose
is old: we strip, paint, varnish,
smooth, and fill its rooms
with other people's antiques. Tiny white
christening gowns and newspaper
clippings sleep in the cedar
chest at the foot of our bed. We bring

in the new year with cranberry punch
and oyster stew. In my tin-plated kitchen
I bake bread, kneading dough
with floured fingers, releasing
yeast quietly as air
between every crevice
of the house, filling the children
with its heavy scent.

Mother's Love

She carried him
like a cat between her teeth
since he could breathe and before:
from the moment she learned
of him-to-be she held him
in the palm of her hand, measuring
him by the size of her belly,
watching his heels kick
against skin stretched so tight
she feared he would rip through,
a Jack-in-the-Pulpit
bursting forth into air.
Finally forceps, and then pulled
awake from her ether dream
to the slap of one nun's bare white hand,
his cry fragile, then firm, steady. A wail.
          Here.

In the early mornings
she held him in the crook of her arm,
curve of her neck, cushion of lap.
His eyes stayed blue
and his nose grew a proud
royal bump. She traced his eyebrows
and sucked food from his slender fingers,
stitched a quilt, pushed his bike, baked
his cakes, saved his skin again and again.
          All for this:

only to have him
grow up and discard her,
spitting her out like some bitter peel
as he walks down the flagstone steps,
his fine leather boots thumping
one beat ahead of her heart.

Ironing Lessons

Start with a spray of starch on the collar first,
crisp and clean. Listen for the hiss of steam.
Move slowly, she says. Take your time.
The smell of stale sweat rises
beneath the fresh scent of soap. I watch

my mother's efficient fingers
flip and flatten, press and caress:
collar, then front placket,
left side, right,
between buttons, over holes.
sleeves, cuffs, that tricky yoke,
breast pocket.
Spray, steam, smooth, smooth.
Left front, back, right front, smooth.

I itch to take over,
to hear the gargle and sizzle of hot water,
feel the heavy weight of steel.
Careful! says mother. You don't want to scorch it!
Oh, but I do, I do.
I want to spray, steam, smooth, flip, flatten,
press that iron down right in the middle
of the crisp white back until it leaves
a brown brand, a torched tattoo
a visible reminder of my recklessness.
Ruined, I'll wad it up and
hide it in the attic, buried deep, deep
in the bottom of a cardboard box.

Boneless Skinless

What does it mean
to throw away a sliver of soap?
How many years must an empty
container be saved? She can't
bring herself to wear an apron
or to save the chicken broth
to use as soup stock later.
Her refrigerator has no patience
for a single pickle or two stalks
of limp celery. Her skillet refuses
bacon grease; her plants renounce
eggshells and coffee grounds, preferring
squirts of store-bought fertilizer.

Serving up supper
straight from the pan
she feels the pains
of child-guilt, heavy
and familiar as the early dark
of winter afternoons.
Boneless, skinless breasts reek
of idleness; she sways
under the weight
of her mother's earnest face
and the memory of her quick, red
hands gouging out
potato eyes.

Letter to the Man I Didn't Marry

Today I ran three yellow lights,
which in some states signal the driver
to *clear the intersection* and in others
to *proceed with caution.* I did
neither, as I'm sure you recall. I hear
you've been asking about me.

My baby knocks more insistently
these days, especially after I eat what's bad
for me: chips or chocolate, late night
bowl of sweetened cereal. (You disapprove,
I know. I remember the angle of your head.)
Maybe she will look like me. Maybe she
will be a he. My breasts grew larger
while I napped. When I opened my eyes,
my son was there to kiss my cheek
with his tiny chapped lips.

From the front porch swing
I watch the librarian fly by on her bike
like the wicked witch and the irises rise
inch by inch. I am itching
to get my hands in the soil, to smell the dirt
caked thick and dark beneath my nails.
You were wrong, you know. You never
could have been the one
to heal me.

Penance

—for Bryan

I kneel to you
in absolution: Forgive me, lover,
for I have sinned. It has been three days
since I last thought of you, over two months
since I spoke

your name aloud. I brought you
these flowers from my mother's garden:
lavender, statice, Michaelmas daisies.
She still can't remember

your name; I have stopped
reminding her. You used to come to me
in dreams; once floating
outside a second-story window
you beckoned. I stepped back,
then awoke, nervous and guilty.

For years now
I've carried the burden of you
like a secret child; I have not spoken
often enough of what it was to know
you. I can't remember

your birthday—is it the third or fifth? By now
your hair would be thinning and your mustache
thick. Your twin brother is bald and bitter;
you will never face his fate.
It's only his voice

that throws me, raspy and cracked,
like yours. And his lips.
I have had impure thoughts.

This is what your mother said to me,
here in this spot, as she handed me your casket's
blue ribbon: *you were the love of his life.*
Have mercy on me,
I have never visited her, but the ribbon fit
nicely in the depths

of my wedding bouquet. Seven years now
I have been married to a man you
never knew, two children who look
like him. I must have forgotten
how, in the pain of afterdeath, I swore
I would name my son for you.

It's all coming back to me now.
Your crooked teeth and bony knees.

The Botanist and His Wife

can't take a walk around the block
without a game of identification. He points:
She: Maple.
He: Yes, but which kind?
She (shrugging): Sugar? Red?
He (sighing): *Acer saccharinum.* Silver maple.
See how the bark peels and how the lobes
of the leaves are jagged and deep?
She (sidestepping): Watch out for the dog—.
Never mind.

First day of spring he kills plants,
sending the philodendron and the African violet out
to sun on the porch, imagining
their chloroplastic ecstasy.
Instead
their leaves are scorched, crisp
as potato chips around the edges.
She: Stay away from my plants. Don't dip
your fingers in my flower beds.
He (head hanging): Well, I just thought—
She (arms akimbo): And don't go near the
garden, either.

(where he pulls the stems off onions, picks
cucumbers before the prickers have softened,
lets zucchini grow monstrous
like some forbidden radioactive experiment)

Daughter

Her cord is still thick and strong
between us; our breathing matches
two for one, two for one. Her cheeks,
forehead, the curve of her nose.
She is mine, still: hearing a rustle
outside she rushes to me and settles.

I must find the blue china
cups of my childhood and share sweet,
hot tea in the mornings while the sun crisps
the maples. I could open a window; we'd breathe
in the thick green leaves of the mountain
laurels, dream of nesting under a tangle
of branches, sunlight seeping here and there.

Last time we camped the full moon rose
above the mountains and lit our tent like a streetlight.
She slept on under dogwood thick with red autumn
berries, breathing in and out the soporific
potion of ragweed and oaks and good red earth.

Dad, Peeling Apples

       The color of wheat
bread speckled
like the skin of a Golden Delicious,
freckles on top of freckles
and tiny nicks
from his knife, dots of blood
turned to brown scabs.
My father's hands

have never changed. Every night
a different apple
skinned naked,
split and seeded without him
ever looking down, loving the fit

of apple
in the left hand, brown-handled
knife in the right.
He licks the tip of his finger
where the juice runs clear
and skewers a slice

for me, which I take
regardless
of whether I want
an apple or whether
the flesh has begun to brown
around the edges.

When he is done,
knife set down and fingers wiped
clean against the legs
of his beige corduroys, I will take
the leathered back
of his hand to my cheek
and hold it there, begging

his weathered roots to spread
their soil-caked fingers
long and strong
as deep as the generations will go.

Seventeen Hours, Give or Take
(Driving South)

We count on someday,
coffee on the front porch,
Buffalo Mountain still

in its own black shadow.
We live now
for the next vacation
and the next, driving southeast
and then south and east,
shedding
these strange selves

as the farms turn to forests,
corn to tobacco.
Two hours to go
and we are easy again
as if some lethal spell
has been lifted. We unzip

our stiff suits
at the state line
and toss them out the window.
Our skin beneath is warm

and smells greenly of wood.
We can't stop breathing.

Spring on Chestnut Top

I long to lie
in the thick apple moss,
hemmed in by doghobble,
leafy liverwort at my feet,
lichen like a lacy pillow under my head,
covered by a canopy of sugar
maple and red buckeye,
butterfly ghosts of beech leaves
fluttering above.

If I were very, very quiet,
would I bear witness
to the resurrection fern's curls
awakening?
Could I hear the fiddlehead
slowly unfurling
and the bloodroot whispering:
It's time! It's time!

Would I see fire pink
blink open beneath the ledge,
standing guard like a good shepherd
over its flock of seersucker sedge
and sweet white trillium?

Listen!
The winter wren whistles its welcome:
Awaken, Awaken!
It shakes and scampers from log to leaf,
leaf to log,
a trembling, ecstatic greeter.

Where Emily Leapt

I am searching for the exact spot
where Emily leapt over the creek, a tiny wood

nymph beneath silverbells and sugar maples,
behind her a hundred shades of green:

moss and ferns and brook lettuce,
hemlocks and buckeyes and tulip trees

just leafing out, so tender you could sprinkle them
in your salad and savor spring's first breath.

We were all young then and laughing,
cameras snapping and snacks in our backpacks,

jackets already discarded and shoelaces retied, shouting
warnings to the children about roots and rocks and sharp edges.

I'll never find it again, that perfect field of wildflowers
where Emily landed laughing on her two small feet

bare in a lush mass of fringed phacelia and sweet white trillium,
the sun sprinkling glitter on her floating white dress.

Strawberry Moon in June

10:40 & the moon hides coyly just out of sight
behind the black hump of Horseshoe Ridge,
taking its own sweet time, a slow rise, a tease
barely outlining the trees. I squeeze your hand, dark
blind: we will have no street-light bright moonlit path
shining along Sparks Lane tonight.

Fireflies, though: those sparkling fairies
light the way this hot black summer night.
A thousand thousand dazzling dancers
Sweating in white-hot disco ball frenzy:
Flashing their hellos, looking for love,
illuminating their essence.
   I'm here.
      I'm here.
    I'm here.
        Pick me.

Coming Out of the Den

On the west prong
of the Little Pigeon we rest:
this is no stream whispering
in the woods but a boiling cauldron,
a whirlpool sparking diamond
whitecaps of cascades, swirling
and bubbling with ferocity:
  Let me free! Let me flow!
Sure of where she is going,
this full-bodied daughter
of a greater river shoulders
on, bullies past boulders
and branches.

  We shed boots and socks,
stretch winter weary toes. Open
arms up and out, root feet, faces
to blue sky, river ravishing
all around us. Somewhere in the woods
a water thrush gurgles;
the brush thrashes: bear maybe,
or just a squirrel. You kneel
by the mayapple and lift a leaf
of wild ginger: beneath, a patch
of brook lettuce glitters greenly.
  Sunlight sifts
through fresh beech leaves, shaking
sparkles onto the moss
beneath our bare feet.
Our tongues catch
sunflakes; we gulp cups of gold,
swallowing spring.

Life Cycle

September's cicadas are in a frenzy of crescendo
and diminuendo, their sound boxes like kettle drums,

tymbals flexing in celebration and lament, buckling
and unbuckling, ridges rubbing faster and faster, drumstick

clicks on washboard: We've done it, they cry! We've met
and married; mating's done; our progeny buried in bark

to emerge next summer or maybe in seventeen, tiny nymphs
that slept through our deaths, never knew how the song

rose and fell one last time that late summer day. How fast
it all transpired once we fed and left our old skins behind.

Driving Up Unaka Mountain

That October the wild roses wove
their way through the barbed wire
fence. Your first time in the mountains.
You stood on the edge for so long I stopped
breathing, thinking you would stretch out
your arms and dive into the green and yellow
and orange below. Or maybe I would
try it myself, not for death but for the sheer joy
of being part of something so absolute,
catching your hand as I leapt,
leaving you

laughing gap-toothed and loud.
Instead we found a warm rock
and read the books we'd brought along.
I studied the tiny freckles of your skin,
and thought about ways
to make you stay.

I was never hungry
then. Now I would pack a basket
of baguettes and brie and grapes.
Now I would be a tourist. The old people
on their porches would see my out-of-state
license plates and turn their heads, blinking

away my wave. At the top I would raise
a glass of wine and photograph the view,
everything edged and cornered.

My father picks apples in the snow

What started
as flurries now whips
wildly around him.
Late October, and the Mutsus
will be lost in the freeze.
He picks with the twist
of wrist that all apple pickers
do in their autumnal sleep.
My father smells
of apples. Has always
smelled of apples.
His hands are nicked, freckled
and scabbed; he places
each apple in the basket,
loving each one.

My father picks apples
as the snow swirls,
sweeps through the branches
of Winesaps and Northern Spies:
Packed in a parka,
all sound muffled by furred ear flaps,
he fairly dances between the rows,
through whirling white
with the bittersharp scent
steeped deep in his skin—
a million dreams of hard-pressed cider
releases: seed, skin, pulp,
juice.

Rock of Ages

Our mother
sheds old age piece by piece:
Hearing aids dropped, camouflaged on mottled
beige carpet until the vacuum cleaner finds them,
rattling in the hose like copper pennies.

Metal walker left behind on the farm's front porch,
Hidden behind apple crates, ping pong paddles,
boots, a string of lights, bikes, gloves, sweatshirts,
as jumbled as the junkyard she loved so much as a child.

Who knows when
the slick shepherd's crook of a cane went missing?
Probably wedged behind a doorway, stuck in the car trunk,
propped against the poplar tree, or dangling from a shopping
cart's cracked handle at the supermarket.

The bifocals are last to go, finally found folded
atop the piano behind a framed photo of herself at twenty-one
beneath apple blossoms, gazing skyward.
She must have been playing there, fingers fumbling nimbly
across the keys, chords of memory deep and wide—

She knows how this old hymn goes,
and that it goes on and on and on, verse by verse,
the joyous harmonious chorus repeating,
ending at last with an all-out
lusty threefold Amen.

Unstitched

I am held together
by tiny stitches
on small scraps of feed sack,
snatches of wool, snips of gingham.
A patchwork of pastels—
a slipshod collage of cotton.
I've been silk, satin, taffeta;
I've been flowers, polka-dots, and plaid.

Thin white thread
                    zig-zags
        across
                    the decades
        hemming me in, keeping me
from ripping.

I've been zipped.
        Buttoned.
                    Unsnapped.
I've been bumblebunched, twisted,
and straightened. Held pins in my mouth,
pricked fingers, and calloused
my thimble-less thumbs.

I am done.
Unravel me now:
Rip out the seams
one by one, untwist strings
and untangle knots. Fold me gently.
What I haven't finished—
take now.
Begin again.

Sarah Cummins Small is originally from the Finger Lakes region of New York. She now lives and writes with a view of the Smoky Mountains near Knoxville, TN, where she and her husband raised their three children. For over 20 years, Small taught creative writing, literature, and composition to students at all levels, from elementary to college. Her award-winning poetry has appeared in *Appalachia Bare, Cider Press Review, Tiny Wren Lit, Yalobusha Review*, and *Willawaw Journal*, among others, as well as in the anthologies *Breathing the Same Air* and *Migrants and Stowaways*. She holds an MA in English/creative writing from Iowa State University. *Stitches* is her first chapbook.